LITTLE PARTY BOOKS
ADVENTURE

contents

jungle beat

If you want to give your little Tarzan or Jane something to roar about, we've created a celebration that is sure to bring out the party animal in everyone. Free the kids from captivity, embark on a safari adventure (it is best to hold this party outdoors in a garden or a park), and watch the little monkeys go totally wild.

invitation

These lizard invitations with their cheeky pink tongues are fun to receive and set the scene for the jungle party.

you will need
(makes 6 invitations)

thin cardboard, for the templates
scissors
3 sheets dark green A4 paper
1 sheet bright green A4 paper
1 sheet bright pink A4 paper
scissors (we used craft scissors with
    a scalloped edge for the leaves)
dark green coloured pencil
self-adhesive paper dots, optional
glue stick
white pen

Using the picture, opposite, as a guide, draw a freehand lizard (or trace one from a book), about 13cm long, onto the thin template cardboard; cut out template. Draw a freehand leaf (about 14cm long) onto the cardboard making sure that one edge is flat (to fold the invitation); cut out template.

To make the leaf, fold one piece of dark green paper in half lengthways. Match the edge of the leaf template to the fold of the paper; trace around template then cut out leaf from green paper. You will get two invitations from one piece of A4 paper.

Using the bright green paper, trace around lizard template. Decorate the lizard using the coloured pencil and/or self-adhesive dots then cut out.

Draw a long thin tongue (about 5cm) for each lizard on the pink paper; cut out.

Glue the tongue onto the underside of each lizard; glue the lizard onto the right-hand side of the inside of the leaf.

When dry, gently roll the tongue using your thumb and forefinger. Write out the party details on the inside of the leaf using the white pen.

Party us for
join
a Jungle Boat Party
on March 18
at 2pm- 4pm
6 Vine Street, Riverwood
RSVP.

Party

Above Fold paper in
half, trace then cut out
leaves so they join in
the middle.
Opposite Trace lizard
onto light green paper,
decorate as you like,
then cut out.

7

table
decorations

Style the room (or patio) using a bamboo screen (available from gardening and hardware stores). Support a length of dark netting using bamboo poles or, alternatively, wooden dowels could be used.

Use plastic banana-style plates as placemats.

We covered a white table with a runner made of green crepe paper (if you don't have a white table, cover the table with a white tablecloth first). The table was set with disposable bamboo plates and cutlery, which was wrapped in an animal print napkin and tied with twine (available from department and gardening stores). The paper cups are also in a pale bamboo colour. The centrepiece was made from an assortment of large vine leaves (available from florists and garden-supply stores).

dress-uPs

Face-painting kits are available from toy shops and department stores; most come with instructions on how to paint animal faces or you could be inspired by children's picture books.

Once the kids have had their faces painted, complete the look with a set of animal ears. They're really simple to make: just draw the ears of the jungle animals on thin pieces of coloured cardboard, making sure that the ears match their animal faces, then cut out and attach them to a headband (available from craft and party stores). Another easy idea is to make animal tails for the kids to attach to their lower backs. Cut a tail out of cardboard, paint or colour it according to the animal, and safety pin (or peg) it to their clothes.

Painting a splash of colour on the children's faces is sure to be a roaring success. Get some friends involved and paint the kids' faces like tigers, leopards and zebras. You can buy face paint from toy shops and department stores.

A safari hunt, set up in your backyard or nearby park, is a great way to let energetic kids have fun. Things like foil-covered chocolate eggs, plastic animals and other jungle treats, make fantastic treasures. Hide the treasures over the garden or park; be inventive and put them in the roots of trees and under low branches and plants, but make sure they are within reach of the children. Give each child a small basket or bag for their treasures.

activities

All your young explorers will love this cake. The swamp is filled with murky (but delicious) jelly, hiding reptiles and jungle animals.

swamp cake

3 x 340g packets buttercake mix
85g packet purple jelly crystals
85g packet green jelly crystals
green and brown food colouring
48cm round platter or cake board
decorations
fresh violet leaves
assorted toy swamp animals
green jelly snakes
milk chocolate sultanas
red and orange boiled lollies, crushed
30g Flake bar, halved
chocolate leaves
150g white chocolate Melts, melted
25 fresh camellia leaves

1 Preheat oven to 180°C/160°C fan-forced. Grease and line deep 26cm x 36cm baking dish.
2 Make cakes according to packet directions, pour into dish; bake about 1 hour. Stand cake 20 minutes before turning onto wire rack to cool.
3 Make jellies, separately, according to packet directions; pour enough of the purple jelly into the green jelly until it becomes a "swampy" green colour. Refrigerate jelly until set.
4 Use a serrated knife to level cake top; turn cut-side down. Using picture, opposite, as a guide, cut a swamp shape around outside edge of cake.
5 Position cake, cut-side down, on platter. Using picture as a guide, mark a rough outline on the cake for swamp water, about 2cm deep; hollow out area.
6 Using instructions, opposite, make butter cream. Spread butter cream over cake up to the swamp-water line.
7 Using instructions, opposite, make chocolate leaves.
8 Using whisk, break up jelly; spoon into swamp hollow. Position violet leaves on jelly, and animals and snakes on and around cake.
9 Make campfire by using sultanas and crushed boiled lollies. Position Flake for logs near campfire.
10 Make a "no swimming" sign; secure to wooden skewer or ice-block stick, position on cake. Decorate sides of cake with chocolate leaves.

party cake

Butter cream Beat 250g soft butter with electric mixer until as white as possible. Gradually beat in 1½ cups icing sugar and ⅓ cup milk. Beat in an extra 1½ cups icing sugar. Tint a pale green colour.

Chocolate leaves Using green colouring, tint chocolate a pale green colour. Brush chocolate onto back of clean, dry camellia leaves. Set at room temperature then carefully peel leaves away from the chocolate.

Cake can be baked and cut into shape one day ahead; keep, covered, in the refrigerator.

The remaining purple jelly can be used to make extra *snakes-alive jelly cups*, see page 26, if you like.

15

party food

Food is very important to our intrepid explorers; we have jungle slush to combat the heat, then watch as young travellers struggle with snakes trying to slither out of jelly cups. Any jungle explorer needs to face fierce lions, and the cupcakes, topped with delicious chocolate honeycomb, show why lions are kings of the jungle.

jungle slush

preparation time 30 minutes **serves** 12

12 kiwifruit (1kg)
3½ cups ice cubes
3 cups (750ml) chilled kiwi mix
    fruit juice

1   Peel kiwifruit, quarter lengthways; remove core and as many black seeds as possible.
2   Just before serving, blend kiwifruit, ice cubes and juice, in batches, until almost smooth. Pour into large jug to serve.

Use a large piping bag fitted with a large plain tube to pipe the mince mixture onto the pastry.

Rolls can be cooked one day ahead; keep, covered, in the refrigerator.

Reheat rolls in single layer on oven trays, covered loosely with foil, in oven (180°C/160°C fan-forced) for about 15 minutes.

sausage rolls

preparation time 15 minutes **cooking time** 30 minutes **makes** 24

2 teaspoons vegetable oil
1 small brown onion (80g), grated coarsely
1 slice stale white bread, crusts removed
200g sausage mince
200g beef mince
2 teaspoons tomato paste
½ teaspoon dried mixed herbs
1 tablespoon finely chopped fresh flat-leaf parsley
2 sheets ready-rolled puff pastry
1 egg, beaten lightly

1 Preheat oven to 220°C/200°C fan-forced. Line two oven trays with baking paper.

2 Heat oil in small frying pan; cook onion until soft.

3 Dip bread quickly in a small bowl of cold water; discard water.

4 Combine onion and bread in medium bowl with minces, paste, mixed herbs and parsley.

5 Cut pastry sheets in half lengthways. Spoon or pipe mince mixture along centre of each pastry piece. Turn one long side of pastry over mince mixture; brush pastry flap with egg. Turn other long side of pastry over to enclose mince mixture.

6 Cut each roll into six pieces. Place rolls, seam-side down, on trays; brush with egg. Make two cuts in top of each roll; bake rolls about 30 minutes or until browned.

7 Stand 10 minutes before serving with tomato sauce.

Uncooked rolls can be frozen between layers of freezer wrap for up to three months. Or, wrap uncut rolls individually in plastic (we used the plastic that separates the pastry sheets) and freeze in an airtight container for up to three months.

Thaw uncut rolls in the refrigerator for about 12 hours or overnight. Cut and bake as per recipe.

deep-south finger-lickin' wings

preparation time 10 minutes (plus refrigeration time)
cooking time 30 minutes **serves** 4

1kg chicken wings
2 tablespoons tomato sauce
2 tablespoons worcestershire sauce
2 tablespoons brown sugar
1 tablespoon american mustard
dipping sauce
2 tablespoons tomato sauce
1 tablespoon worcestershire sauce
2 tablespoons brown sugar
1 tablespoon american mustard

1 Preheat oven to 220°C/200°C fan-forced.

2 Cut wings into three pieces at joints; discard tips. Combine sauces, sugar and mustard in large bowl. Add chicken; toss chicken to coat in marinade. Cover; refrigerate 3 hours or overnight.

3 Place chicken, in single layer, on oiled wire rack set inside large shallow baking dish; brush remaining marinade over chicken.

4 Roast, uncovered, about 30 minutes or until chicken is well browned and cooked through.

5 Meanwhile, make dipping sauce. Serve chicken wings with sauce.

dipping sauce Combine ingredients in small bowl; cook, covered, in microwave oven on HIGH (100%) for 1 minute.

mexican bagels

preparation time 5 minutes **cooking time** 5 minutes **serves** 2

1 bagel
1 tablespoon bottled tomato salsa
½ small avocado (100g),
  sliced thickly
2 slices cheddar cheese

1 Preheat grill.

2 Split bagel in half horizontally; spread 2 teaspoons of salsa over each half. Top each half with avocado and one cheese slice.

3 Place under grill about 5 minutes or until cheese melts.

Cakes can be made one day ahead; store in an airtight container.

Cakes can be completed up to three hours ahead; keep refrigerated if the weather is hot.

Cooked cakes can be frozen for up to one month. Thaw cakes at room temperature for about three hours.

Serve the cupcakes on a large water lilly leaf (visit your local florist or aquarium centre to enquire if they're available) or make it yourself using dark-green cardboard or a waterproof dark-green fabric.

king of the jungle cupcakes

preparation time 40 minutes   cooking time 20 minutes   makes 12

340g packet buttercake mix
caramel food colouring
butter cream
250g softened butter
3 cups icing sugar
1/3 cup milk
decorations
5 x 50g Violet Crumble bars
1 black licorice strap
24 dark Choc Bits

1   Preheat oven to 180°C/160°C fan-forced; line 12-hole (1/3-cup/80ml) muffin pan with paper cases.
2   Make cake according to packet directions; divide mixture evenly among cases. Bake about 20 minutes. Stand cakes 5 minutes before turning, top-side up, onto wire rack to cool.

3   Meanwhile, make butter cream. Spread cakes with butter cream.
4   Cut Violet Crumble bars into thin shards. Cut licorice strap into 12 small triangles for nose; cut remaining licorice into strips to make whiskers and mouth.
5   Using picture, opposite, as a guide, position licorice on cakes to make face; use Choc Bits for eyes. Use crumble bar shards to make lions' manes.
butter cream Beat butter with electric mixer until as white as possible. Gradually beat in half the sifted icing sugar and milk. Beat in remaining sifted icing sugar. Tint with caramel food colouring.

snakes-alive jelly cups

preparation time 15 minutes (plus refrigeration time) **makes** 12

2 x 85g packets green jelly crystals
12 large jelly snakes
85g packet yellow jelly crystals

1   Make green jelly according to packet directions; cool. Pour jelly evenly among 12 (⅔-cup/160ml) clear plastic cups.

2   Curl one snake into each jelly cup, hanging snake's head over edge of cup. Refrigerate about 3 hours or until jelly is set.

3   Make yellow jelly according to packet directions; cool. Carefully pour yellow jelly over green jelly in cups; refrigerate about 3 hours or until set.

rocky road ice-cream

preparation time 5 minutes **serves** 4

2 x 55g Cherry Ripe bars,
chopped coarsely
50g coloured mallow bakes
2 tablespoons crushed
roasted peanuts
1 litre vanilla ice-cream
⅓ cup chocolate Ice Magic

1 Combine Cherry Ripe, mallow bakes and nuts in medium bowl.
2 Spoon ice-cream into four serving bowls; drizzle ice-cream with Ice Magic then top with Cherry Ripe mixture.
tip Instead of topping the ice-cream with the rocky road, combine the chopped Cherry Ripe and some softened vanilla ice-cream; re-freeze then serve scoops of ice-cream drizzled with Ice Magic.

gingerbread kids

preparation time 30 minutes **cooking time** 10 minutes **makes** 20

125g butter
⅓ cup (75g) firmly packed
   brown sugar
½ cup (175g) golden syrup
3 cups (450g) plain flour
2 teaspoons ground ginger
2 teaspoons ground cinnamon
½ teaspoon ground clove
2 teaspoons bicarbonate of soda
1 egg, beaten lightly
1 teaspoon vanilla extract
royal icing
1 egg white
1 cup (160g) pure icing sugar
food colourings

1 Preheat oven to 180°C/160°C
fan-forced. Lightly grease oven trays.
2 Heat butter, sugar and golden
syrup in small microwave-safe bowl,
uncovered, on HIGH (100%) in
microwave oven about 1 minute or
until butter has melted. Remove bowl
from microwave oven; cool butter
mixture 5 minutes.

3 Sift combined flour, spices and
soda into large bowl; add butter
mixture, egg and extract, stir with
wooden spoon until combined.
4 Knead dough lightly on floured
surface; using a rolling pin, roll dough
into a 5mm thickness. Cut out shapes
using a gingerbread-man cutter; place
shapes on oven trays.
5 Bake, uncovered, about 10 minutes
or until golden brown. Cool on trays.
6 Meanwhile, make royal icing.
Decorate gingerbread kids as you
like with royal icing.
royal icing Beat egg white in small
bowl with electric mixer until just
frothy; gradually add sifted icing
sugar, beating between additions,
until stiff peaks form. Tint icing as
desired, using various food colourings.
tips If the mixture in step 3 is dry and
crumbly, add a little more beaten egg,
just enough to make the dough feel
like play dough.
To make a quick piping bag, cut off
a corner of a small plastic bag; use
this to pipe faces on gingerbread kids.

You obviously need a gingerbread-man cutter to make this shape, but any decorative cutter – a star, diamond, heart or whatever shape you already have in your kitchen – can be used for this recipe.

take-home treats

White paper bags make the perfect vessel to fill with lollies when it comes time to leave the jungle. To make it really authentic, attach some vine or twigs and a large camellia or vine leaf to the top of the bag. Fill the bag with lots of small plastic jungle animals and animal-shaped sweets and, if you like, peg the bags to a tree.

by the sea

Come on, it's time to go down to the sea ...
we're off to the beach where there are plenty
of fish, sea stars and a jellyfish or two. Bring
your fishing rod, bucket and spade, there's
plenty of fun to be had including a fish piñata.
This is a great party to be held outdoors
where little fishermen are free to drop a line.

invitation

These fish invitations are a cute novelty that the younger kids will love and, best of all, they take next-to-no time to make.

you will need

thin cardboard, for the templates · scissors · white cardboard
white A4 paper · poster paints · glue · light blue cardboard
25cm fine silver cord, approximately
24mm diameter self-adhesive paper dots

Draw freehand fish shapes onto the thin template cardboard; cut out shapes. Trace fish template onto white cardboard; decorate as desired. We used white paper that was painted with poster paint, cut into shapes then glued onto the fish (see picture, opposite). Cut out the fish.

Cut out three circles from the blue cardboard, 6cm, 5cm and 4cm in diameter. Write the party details on the front of each "bubble". Attach the cord to the back of each circle with a self-adhesive dot; attach the bottom of the cord to the back of the fish.

Instead of painting the plain paper to decorate the fish, just glue on any coloured paper you have in the house.

table
decorations

Cover the table with a brightly coloured polka-dot tablecloth. Set the table using plastic plates and cutlery the same colours as the tablecloth (check out party shops and discount stores for unusually shaped plates and bowls). Cutlery could be placed on the table in a bucket. A fish piñata is a great centrepiece as it can be used later as a game.

Style the room by hanging blow-up Japanese paper balls or miniature plastic beach balls from the ceiling (suspended by strong fishing line). Check out toy stores and discount stores and visit your local Chinatown or Asian shops. You could also cover the chairs using large beach towels in bright colours.

dress-ups

adventure by the sea

If you like, ask the kids to come
dressed as their favourite sea
creature, such as a shark,
mermaid or King Neptune.
Kids can come dressed in
their favourite summer wear,
or as fishermen, if they like.
You could also fill up a small
inflatable pool with sand to
further add to the theme, and
have prizes for the best sand
castle. Sand is available from
garden outlets, hardware stores
and brick and tile centres.

activities

Make an underwater mural; this is a great way
to get the kids' imaginations working and will
bring out their creative abilities.

underwater mural

you will need

4 sheets white cardboard
thin cardboard, for templates
strong sticky tape or masking tape
different coloured A4 papers · scissors
selection of art materials including
gouache paints; glitter pens; crayons;
coloured pencils · stamps · craft glue

Before the party starts you will need to make the backdrop. To do this, tape the backs of the white cardboard together to make one large piece. **Draw** freehand fish and sea creature shapes onto template cardboard then cut out. Trace templates onto the coloured papers then cut out. **When** it's time to get the kids involved, spread out a selection of art materials; give them the fish shapes to decorate. Once they've finished decorating, you can glue the completed shapes onto the cardboard.

go fish

A fun way to go
fishing at home.

for the fish

large blue cardboard
different coloured
thin cardboard
art materials including
coloured pencils, crayons,
gouache paints, sequins
coloured ribbons and
self-adhesive coloured dots
scissors and paperclips

Cut the blue cardboard
into a pond shape.
Trace the fish and other sea
creature templates you made
for the underwater mural
onto the coloured cardboard.
Decorate the fish using art
materials then cut out shapes.
Using a large self-adhesive dot,
stick a paper clip under the nose
of each fish, leaving the end of
the paper clip protruding slightly.

for the fishing rod

fine sand paper
50cm x 9.55mm dowel
white and coloured acrylic paints
75cm twine
small magnet (available from toy shops)

Lightly sand the ends of the dowel; undercoat using the white acrylic paint. When dry, paint the fishing rod the colour of your choice.

Tie a small magnet onto the end of the twine and tie the other end onto the rod, about 3cm from the end.

To play, place the pond on the floor and all the fish on top; sit the children in a circle around the pond. Each child takes a turn with the rod and tries to catch a fish. To make it more interesting for older children, write a number underneath each fish, and the person with the highest (or lowest) amount of points at the end of the game is the winner.

Make extra fish for the kids to decorate while they are doing the mural. These fish can be used for the fishing game.

Draw the fish onto the cardboard and make the fishing rod before the day of the party so you're not pressed for time on the day.

If you like, make a fishing rod for each child to take home with them. Write the child's name on a fish; attach it to the rod and use it on the table as a place name.

The kids will just love this happy smiling jellyfish cake. Floating in blue jelly, and with rainbow straps for tentacles, it is really eye catching and, best of all, can be made the day before and assembled on the day of the party.

jellyfish

2 x 340g packets buttercake mix
4 x 85g packets blue jelly crystals
decorations
1 white marshmallow, halved widthways
1 egg shell, halved, washed, dried
2 blue Smarties
9 rainbow straps
fish lollies
raspberries lollies
plastic coral

1   Preheat oven to 180°C/160°C fan-forced; grease and line deep 26cm x 33cm baking dish.
2   Make cake according to packet directions, pour into dish; bake about 1 hour. Stand cake 20 minutes; turn, top-side up, onto wire rack to cool.
3   Dissolve jellies in large heatproof bowl using 3 cups (750ml) boiling water and 2½ cups (625ml) cold water. Refrigerate until set.

4   Using serrated knife, level top of cake; turn cut-side down. Using picture, opposite, as a guide, cut jellyfish shape from cake. Place in 35cm x 45cm plastic tray (if it's metal, line with foil).
5   Make butter cream (see right); spread all over cake.
6   Cut two hollows for jellyfish's eye sockets. Place marshmallow halves into each egg shell; secure Smarties to marshmallows with a little butter cream. Position eyes on cake. Cut a blue strip from one rainbow strap; position on cake for jellyfish's mouth.
7   Using whisk, break up jelly; spoon carefully into tray around cake.
8   Using picture as a guide, position remaining rainbow straps as tentacles. Decorate jelly with raspberries, fish and coral.

party cake

Butter cream Beat 250g soft butter with electric mixer until as white as possible. Gradually beat in 1½ cups icing sugar and ⅓ cup milk. Beat in an extra 1½ cups icing sugar. Use food colouring to tint butter cream green.

Cooked cake can be frozen for up to one month. Thaw cake at room temperature for about six hours.

Jelly and cake can be completed a day ahead. Refrigerate separately.

Position cake, tentacles and decorations in tray up to three hours ahead. Refrigerate if weather is hot.

Plastic coral is available from toy shops and pet stores.

party food

Jelly can be made a day ahead; store, covered, in the refrigerator.

Down to the sea we go, with jelly sea stars **in lemonade, torpedoes and, of course, fish** and chips. Make more fish and chips for **older, hungrier children, if you like, and** don't forget the tomato sauce.

sea star lemonade

preparation time 15 minutes (plus refrigeration time) **serves** 12

3 x 85g packets blue jelly crystals
2 cups (500ml) boiling water
3 litres (12 cups) chilled lemonade

1 Line 20cm x 30cm lamington pan with plastic wrap.
2 Place jelly crystals in large heatproof jug, add the boiling water; stir until crystals are dissolved. Pour jelly into pan; refrigerate 3 hours or until set.
3 Turn jelly onto board, remove plastic; cut out 12 x 6cm stars.
4 Just before serving, place stars in glasses; gently pour in lemonade.

bacon and corn dip

preparation time 5 minutes **cooking time** 5 minutes **makes** 2¼ cups

4 rindless bacon rashers (260g),
  finely chopped
250g softened packaged
  cream cheese
300g can creamed corn
¼ cup (60g) sour cream
4 green onions, sliced thinly

1 Cook bacon in small frying pan until crisp; drain on absorbent paper.

2 Beat cream cheese in small bowl with electric mixer until smooth.

3 Stir in bacon, creamed corn, sour cream and green onions.

tip Serve with your choice of savoury biscuits or bagel toasts.

mini pizza torpedoes

preparation time 15 minutes **cooking time** 10 minutes **serves** 12

12 "bake at home" bread rolls

½ cup (125ml) tomato pasta sauce

1½ cups (180g) coarsely grated
cheddar cheese

5 slices (25g) mild salami,
chopped coarsely

10 seeded black olives,
chopped finely

3 green onions, chopped finely

100g leg ham, chopped finely

⅓ cup drained canned
crushed pineapple

1 Preheat oven to 200°C/180°C fan-forced.

2 Cut each roll in half lengthways.

3 Place rolls on oven tray, cut-side-up; spread each half with sauce. Top with half the cheese.

4 Sprinkle 6 rolls with salami, olives and half the onion. Sprinkle remaining rolls with ham, pineapple and remaining onion. Top rolls with remaining cheese.

5 Bake about 10 minutes or until cheese has melted.

fish & chips

preparation time 35 minutes **cooking time** 40 minutes **serves** 12

2kg large oval potatoes, peeled
cooking-oil spray
12 firm white fish fillets (1.2kg)
¼ cup (35g) plain flour
1 egg
¼ cup (60ml) milk
1 cup (70g) stale breadcrumbs
½ cup (80g) corn flake crumbs

1 Preheat oven to 200°C/180°C fan-forced.
2 Cut potatoes into 1.5cm slices; cut slices into 1cm chips. Place chips, in single layer, on oiled oven tray; spray with oil. Cook, uncovered, about 40 minutes or until chips are browned and tender.
3 Meanwhile, cut each fillet into three pieces. Toss pieces in flour, shake off excess; dip pieces in combined egg and milk then toss in combined crumbs. Place pieces on oiled oven tray; spray with oil.
4 Bake fish, uncovered, for the final 15 minutes of chip baking time.

Fish can be crumbed, ready for baking, up to three hours ahead of cooking time; keep, covered, in the refrigerator.

Potatoes can be prepared up to three hours ahead of cooking time; keep, covered, in water. Drain and dry potatoes well before cooking.

layered banana split with caramel sauce

preparation time 10 minutes **cooking time** 10 minutes **serves** 4

⅔ cup (160ml) thickened cream
60g butter
¾ cup (165g) firmly packed
  brown sugar
1 cup (250ml) thickened cream, extra
500ml vanilla ice-cream
2 large bananas (460g),
  sliced thinly
½ cup (40g) almond flakes, toasted

1 Stir cream, butter and sugar in small saucepan, over medium heat, until smooth. Reduce heat; simmer, uncovered, 2 minutes. Cool 10 minutes.
2 Meanwhile, beat extra cream in small bowl with electric mixer until soft peaks form.
3 Divide half of the sauce among four serving dishes; top with ice-cream, cream, banana, remaining sauce and nuts.

orange butterscotch fondue

preparation time 20 minutes **cooking time** 10 minutes **serves** 6

⅔ cup (150g) firmly packed
  brown sugar
25g butter
⅔ cup (160ml) cream
1 teaspoon finely grated orange rind
2 tablespoons orange juice
100g white eating chocolate,
  chopped coarsely
1 large banana (230g),
  chopped coarsely
250g strawberries, halved
2 small pears (360g),
  chopped coarsely
2 medium mandarins (400g),
  segmented
18 marshmallows

1 Stir sugar, butter, cream, rind and juice in medium saucepan until sugar dissolves. Bring to a boil; boil, uncovered, 3 minutes. Remove from heat; cool 5 minutes.

2 Stir in chocolate until fondue mixture is smooth; stand 5 minutes. Transfer to serving bowl.

3 Arrange fruit and marshmallows on serving platter; serve with fondue and skewers for dipping.

tip Prepare fruit just before serving so that it doesn't turn brown or dry out.

frozen fruit and yogurt blocks

preparation time 5 minutes (plus freezing time) **makes** 6

1½ cups (420g) vanilla yogurt
1 cup (150g) frozen mixed berries
1 tablespoon honey

1 Combine yogurt, berries and honey in medium bowl; spoon into six ¼-cup (60ml) ice-block moulds. Press lids on firmly; freeze overnight.

take-home treats

A super surprise for the beachcombers to take home is a small beach bucket filled with marine-themed toys, games and sweets. Make a name tag out of cardboard in the shape of a fish, and tie it onto the handle of the bucket with some string.

If they like, kids can also take home any fish they caught in the "go fish" game, and their fishing rod, to show mum and dad how good they are at fishing.

Young children love bold colours and these small buckets certainly are. The beach balls tied to the ceiling can also be added to the take-home treats. There are all sorts of marine animals available from toy shops, discount stores, party shops and pet stores (in the fish section). Also add any fish lollies left over from the party cake.

index

Food

B
bacon and corn dip 50
bagels, mexican 22
banana split with caramel
  sauce, layered 57
butterscotch orange fondue 58

C
cake, jellyfish party 46
cake, swamp party 14
chicken wings (deep-south
  finger-lickin' wings) 21
chips & fish 54
corn and bacon dip 50
cupcakes, king of the jungle 25

D
dip, bacon and corn 50
dipping sauce 21
drinks
  jungle slush (kiwifruit) 17
  sea star lemonade 49

F
fish & chips 54
fondue, orange butterscotch 58
fruit and yogurt blocks, frozen 61

G
gingerbread kids 30

I
ice-cream, rocky road 29
icing, royal 30

J
jelly cups, snakes-alive 26
jellyfish party cake 46
jungle slush (kiwifruit) 17

L
lemonade, sea star 49

M
mexican bagels 22
mini pizza torpedoes 53

O
orange butterscotch fondue 58

P
party cake, jellyfish cake 46
party cake, swamp cake 14
pizza torpedoes, mini 53

R
rocky road ice-cream 29
royal icing 30

S
sauce, dipping 21
sausage rolls 18
sea star lemonade 49
slush, jungle (kiwifruit) 17
snakes-alive jelly cups 26
swamp party cake 14

Y
yogurt and fruit frozen blocks 61

General

activities
face painting 12
treasure hunt 12
underwater mural 42
go fish game 44
fish 44
fishing rod 44

dress-ups
jungle beat 10
by the sea 40

invitations
lizard 6
fish 36

table decorations
jungle beat 8
by the sea 38

take-home treats
jungle beat 32
by the sea 62

TEST KITCHEN
Food director Pamela Clark
ACP BOOKS
General manager Christine Whiston
Editorial director Susan Tomnay
Creative director Hieu Chi Nguyen
Designer Hannah Blackmore
Director of sales Brian Cearnes
Marketing manager Bridget Cody
Business analyst Ashley Davies
Operations manager David Scotto
International rights enquiries Laura Bamford
lbamford@acpuk.com

acp books

ACP Books are published by ACP Magazines
a division of PBL Media Pty Limited
Group publisher, Women's lifestyle
Pat Ingram
Director of sales, Women's lifestyle
Lynette Phillips
Commercial manager, Women's lifestyle
Seymour Cohen
Marketing director, Women's lifestyle
Matthew Dominello
Public relations manager, Women's lifestyle
Hannah Deveraux
Creative director, Events, Women's lifestyle
Luke Bonnano
Research Director, Women's lifestyle
Justin Stone
ACP Magazines, Chief Executive officer
Scott Lorson
PBL Media, Chief Executive officer Ian Law
Produced by ACP Books, Sydney.
Published by ACP Books,
a division of ACP Magazines Ltd,
54 Park St, Sydney; GPO Box 4088,
Sydney, NSW 2001
phone (02) 9282 8618 fax (02) 9267 9438.
acpbooks@acpmagazines.com.au
www.acpbooks.com.au
Printed by Dai Nippon in Korea.
Australia Distributed by Network Services,
phone +61 2 9282 8777 fax +61 2 9264 3278
networkweb@networkservicescompany.com.au
United Kingdom Distributed by Australian
Consolidated Press (UK),
phone (01604) 642 200 fax (01604) 642 300
books@acpuk.com
New Zealand Distributed by Netlink Distribution
Company, phone (9) 366 9966 ask@ndc.co.nz
South Africa Distributed by PSD Promotions,
phone (27 11) 392 6065/6/7 fax (27 11) 392
6079/80 orders@psdprom.co.za
Canada Distributed by Publishers Group Canada
phone (800) 663 5714 fax (800) 565 3770
service@raincoast.com

Title: Little party books adventure : the Australian
women's weekly / editor, Pamela Clark.
Publisher: Sydney : ACP Books, 2008.
ISBN: 978-186396-806-5 (pbk.)
Notes: Includes index.
Subjects: Children's parties. Cookery. Entertaining.
Adventure and adventurers.
Other Authors/Contributors: Clark, Pamela.
Also Titled: Australian women's weekly
Dewey Number: 793.21
© ACP Magazines Ltd 2008 ABN 18 053 273 546
This publication is copyright. No part of it may be
reproduced or transmitted in any form without the
written permission of the publishers.
Selected from the *Kids' Perfect Party Book*
published 2007.